A PERFECT PEACE

NEWMAN: SAINT FOR OUR TIME

A PERFECT PEACE

Newman
Saint for Our Time

Bishop Fintan Monahan

VERITAS

Published 2019 by Veritas Publications
7-8 Lower Abbey Street, Dublin 1, Ireland
publications@veritas.ie
www.veritas.ie

ISBN 978-1-84730-934-1

10 9 8 7 6 5 4 3 2 1

A catalogue record for this book is available from the British Library.

The front cover features a painting of Saint John Henry Newman by Agnieszka Ryan. The original is on display in the Saint John Henry Newman room, Westbourne, Ennis, Co. Clare.

Designed by Lir Mac Cárthaigh
Printed in Ireland by SPRINT-Print Ltd, Dublin

CONTENTS

FOREWORD

Pope Francis believes strongly in the power of saints to encourage and accompany us along our pilgrim path as Christians. In the six years since his election he has canonised almost twice as many saints as St John Paul II did in the entirety of his twenty-seven year pontificate. In *Gaudete et Exultate* (2018), his apostolic exhortation on the call to holiness in today's world, Francis cites Benedict XVI who said, 'Surrounded, led and guided by the friends of God ... I do not have to carry alone what, in truth, I could never carry alone. All the saints of God are there to protect me, to sustain me and to carry me' (4).

Sometimes we struggle to see saints as approachable companions along our pilgrim path. It can be difficult to identify with people who lived centuries ago and in cultural contexts very different to our own. In addition, too often the sinfulness, weakness and failings that are inevitably part of human life have been airbrushed from the accounts we receive of them. The lives presented to us seem so utterly heroic that, instead of feeling encouraged by them, we can experience a sense of dejection.

However, Pope Francis has brought sanctity back down to earth and taught us to recognise holiness in the ordinary struggles of everyday life. He says:

> I like to contemplate the holiness present in the patience of God's people: in those parents who raise their children with immense love, in those men and women who work hard to support their families, in the sick, in elderly religious who never lose their smile. In their daily perseverance I see the holiness of the Church militant. Very often it is a holiness found in our next door neighbours, those who, living in our midst, reflect God's presence. (*GE*, 7)

At the same time, he stresses that he wants us to be encouraged by those who rose to extraordinary challenges in the circumstances in which they found themselves. Referring to St Teresa Benedicta of the Cross, otherwise known as Edith Stein, martyred by the Nazis in a concentration camp during World War II, he invites us to be inspired by saints who, in her words, 'step forth out of the darkest night' (*GE*, 8) in faithful and self-sacrificing witness to God's love.

In St John Henry Newman we get the best of both worlds, so to speak. We find a saint who experienced the same struggles and temptations that we all have to face. At the same time we find someone who had an extraordinary capacity to transform 'the darkest night' into moments of conversion in which he discovered God's grace and deepened his trust in the mystery of God's hidden but ever-present love.

A Perfect Peace captures very well both aspects of Newman: his ordinariness and extraordinariness. As

Bishop Monahan notes, Newman had a serious brush with illness at the age of fifteen, and throughout his life sickness and bodily infirmity were never too far away from him. His family suffered serious financial difficulties and this impacted heavily upon him. He suffered exhaustion and a nervous collapse in his twenties and did badly in his university examinations, barely getting through when he should have got first class honours. Seemingly not great at pacing himself, in the course of his ministry he sometimes suffered exhaustion from overwork and had to take enforced breaks in order to recover.

His brother Charles became an atheist and they rarely saw eye to eye. One of his sisters died suddenly and unexpectedly and for years he found grief at her loss difficult to bear. When he converted to Catholicism he lost many of his friends, and family members distanced themselves from him. He often had to deal with serious misrepresentation in public debate and suffered greatly from a two-year-long libel action, which he lost. One of his major projects, the establishment of a Catholic university in Ireland (1851–8), ended in failure.

We are told by one of Newman's biographers, Maisie Ward, that by the end of 1863 Newman was 'feeling very old, leading a life of almost complete seclusion, dwelling much on the past, believing that his life was ended and that it had in the main been a failure.'[1] Yet he was to have a quarter of a century of life still before him – most of which was fruitful and peaceful – and the last ten years of which he lived as a cardinal.

We each have to choose individually whether or not to place the talents God has given us at his service. A brilliant intellect, such as Newman's, for instance, can lead to sanctity, or it might not. As Bishop Monahan tells us, Newman's foundational moment of 'religious awakening' came at the young age of fifteen. Left at his boarding school for the summer because of the collapse of his father's bank, and suffering ill-health, he immersed himself in reading influential atheistic philosophers such as David Hume (1711–76). At first he found their arguments impressive. The faith he had inherited and had never questioned until then seemed inadequate when confronted with their taunts and challenges. Later he would write, 'I grant … that mere hereditary faith, in those who can have an intelligent faith, is, to say the least, dangerous and inconsistent; nay, in the case of a religious person, rather I would even affirm that it is impossible.'[2]

Under the guidance of a young teacher/pastor this first challenge to his faith became a moment when God was revealed to him more deeply and personally than he had imagined possible heretofore and the legacy of this encounter was a trust in God's providence that stayed with him for the rest of his life. The many beautiful prayers and quotations that Bishop Monahan has shared with us in this book can be read as him sharing with us his personal dialogue with God *de profundis*. My personal favourite is 'The Mission of my Life' ('God has created me to do him some definite service …' [see p. 84]).

We mentioned that saints can seem remote from our experience because their context was very different to ours. Bishop Monahan helps us to realise that this is not the case with St John Henry Newman. He disciplined and channeled his extraordinary intellect into God's service in order to address the questions of his age with conviction and courage. Those questions remain our questions too. Like Newman, for instance, we face a truncation of reason, a reduction of what is considered rational to what is considered scientifically verifiable. Newman challenges this diminished understanding of reason with extraordinary cogency and expertise, presenting faith not only as reasonable and logical but even as compelling. It is not his intellect alone or his faith alone but the way that they work together that makes Newman truly, as Bishop Monahan says, 'a saint for our time'.

At the end of the day there is only one question we need to ask about a spiritual text such as *A Perfect Peace*: does it help in leading us to Christ? This timely introduction to St John Henry Newman more than meets that criterion and we owe Bishop Monahan a debt of gratitude for providing it to us as we celebrate Newman's canonisation.

Éamonn Conway

1. M. Ward (ed.), 'Introduction', *Apologia Pro Vita Sua*, p. v.
2. Paper of 12 January 1860, in Holmes (ed.), *The Theological Papers of John Henry Newman on Faith and Certainty*, p. 86.

INTRODUCTION

'To live is to change, and to be perfect is to have changed often.'

John Henry Newman

John Henry Newman is a new saint of the Catholic Church. A saint is a man or woman who is recognised as having an outstanding degree of holiness, likeness or closeness to God. Saints are made by official Church declaration or by popular acclamation (a folk saint). Newman may fit into both categories because of the impact he made on the teachings of the Catholic Church and the popular appeal of his devotional writings.

Relevance Today

Given his innate wisdom, peerless intellect, deep compassion and profound love for the Lord, there are so many ways in which John Henry Newman can connect with Christians today. Well over a century after his death, we are drawn to Newman as a religious leader, a writer, an educator, a theologian and a philosopher. Whether through our spiritual reading, through our faith, in our understanding of theology, as an inspiration for our prayer lives or as a resource for liturgists, St John Henry Newman speaks to us now, just as he did our forebears.

Newman was a gifted preacher, a dedicated pastor and a tireless worker for the poor in the parishes he served. There would seem to be something for everyone in Newman's vast body of correspondence, his works of theology, devotion, poetry, novels and scholarship.

Personal Appeal

I was first introduced to John Henry Newman as a seminarian, enthusiastically working my way through the spiritual classics. I was very taken by Newman's *Apologia* – his life story. For me it ranks up there with St Augustine's *Confessions*, St Teresa of Ávila's *Interior Castle*, St Thérèse of Lisieux's *The Story of a Soul* and Thomas Merton's *The Seven Storey Mountain* as a memoir of spiritual awakening. I loved Newman's writing style, his clarity, the way almost every sentence was dotted with scriptural allusions, all drawing the reader in a subtle way towards the spiritual and theological mystery in which he was so immersed – a mystery he was anxious to share with his readers. It is little wonder that one biographer described him as a 'master of musical English prose' and 'one of the liveliest letter writers of the Victorian era'.[1]

Saints Today

The image of the 'hero' or visionary has been part of people's lives since time immemorial and remains important for society today. Heroes serve to inspire us by showing that the extraordinary is possible. Saints shine a light in order to show us a clearer pathway to God and we benefit from their example and guidance; they are, in a sense, the heroes and heroines of our faith lives. John Henry Newman has much to teach us in this respect and we certainly need that today.

Newman's Legacy

John Henry Newman may have been deeply mourned on the occasion of his death; however, in terms of his legacy, he did not leave the Church deprived, having bequeathed an indispensable body of work in which he shared his thoughts on topics including Catholic education, the role of the laity in the Church, the understanding of conscience and papal infallibility.

Many have observed that he sowed the seeds for much of the thinking that was to emerge in the Second Vatican Council, almost a century after Newman's time. His ability to combine the intellectual, the spiritual, the moral and to make it relevant to the current situation is truly remarkable. It should come as no wonder that he has now been granted the Church's highest accolade of sainthood.

I hope to offer an introduction to this great man's life by looking at some of what he said and wrote throughout the eighty-nine years of his very full life. My intention for writing this short work is to introduce Newman to those who are not already familiar with him. I would also like to offer an opportunity for returning visitors to become reacquainted with his enduring legacy on the occasion of his canonisation.

I hope a happy relationship with our new saint's life and work will develop and endure. Likewise, may it be an added joy for all of us that we may now pray to Newman as a saint for our time.

✠ *Fintan Monahan*

1. Gilley, *Newman and His Age*, p. 3.

PART ONE

Newman's Pre-Conversion Years 1801–1845

Newman was a convert to the Catholic faith. It was a momentous event in his life and it had repercussions for his family, friends, the Church of England that he left and the Roman Catholic Church that he joined in 1845. To understand his life as a convert it is essential to know something of Newman's life prior to his conversion.

Family Background and Early Schooling

John Henry Newman, the eldest of six children, was born on 21 February 1801 in London, to middle-class Anglican parents. His father John was a banker and Jemima, his mother, was of French extraction. They had six children in all – John Henry, Charles Robert, Francis William and daughters Harriet, Jemima and Mary. Family was very important to the young John Henry and he dearly loved his parents and all his siblings.

At the age of seven, in 1808, John Henry was enrolled as a boarder in Great Ealing School, one of the most prestigious public schools in Britain. He had little or no interest in games or sport but excelled academically and had a flair for speech and drama. He was said to be a shy boy devoted to his mother and wise for his age; his fellow pupils looked up to him and often called on him to settle playground disputes.

Family fortunes took a downturn in 1816 due to the collapse of his father's bank. His father found new employment as a brewery manager and the family income was supplemented by the small amount his mother had inherited. The family were not poor, but never regained their former wealth.

Religious Awakening

Aged fifteen, during a period of illness, John Henry underwent a profound religious awakening. His Church of England background meant that, in terms of spiritual education, the emphasis was on the Bible rather than on the sacraments or Church dogma (teachings). However, as a result of his appetite for reading, reflection and prayer – unusual for a boy of his age – he experienced a religious awakening. This resulted in an 'awakening of consciousness' in which Newman experienced God not as on external 'object' of belief but as a profound inner presence. It also inspired him to be open to the dogmas of faith which taught him the core truths of Christianity. A deep understanding of the Holy Trinity and all its effects were characteristic of his new-found enthusiasm for faith and this became real to him in a unique way. He wrote later in his *Apologia* of that awakening:

> From the age of fifteen, dogma has been the fundamental principle of my religion: I know

> no other religion; I cannot enter into the idea of any other sort of religion; religion, as a mere sentiment, is to me a dream and a mockery.[1]

Most of his peers in the Ealing School would have approached their education with a healthy distinction between work and play. Unlike Newman, who didn't partake in sports, their free time was taken up with sports: swimming, cricket, tennis and fives (akin to handball). One senses a boy of creative talent, sensitivity and intelligence who certainly stood out among his contemporaries and, to some extent, apart from them.

Having been exposed to a traditional Anglican approach to religious matters shared by his family and school, his new understanding of the place of dogmas and 'impressionable beliefs' would have set him further apart from his contemporaries. This gave him a better feeling for the Christ of the scriptures and he himself called this effect 'impressionable beliefs'. The effect of this 'awakening' was bound to have profound and far-reaching effects on how his family, close friends, fellow pupils and school staff viewed him.

This period at Ealing was instrumental not only in sowing the seeds for Newman's eventual conversion to Catholicism but in consolidating his ideas on the development of doctrine and theology. The young Newman could never have imagined that the 'awakening' of his adolescence was merely a forerunner to another awakening decades later when, as a man of forty-four, he would be received into the Catholic Church. He had a long way to travel before then. However, it is worth noting an enlightening point made by Oratorian priest Keith Beaumont about Newman's boyhood 'awakening':

> It is even, in fact, in the strict sense of the term, his only conversion, since the original and traditional meaning of the term does not refer to the leaving of one Christian tradition or denomination for another, but to a person's turning towards God.[2]

When we think of Newman we tend to concentrate on his later years and the term 'convert' has defined that period of his life for many of us. However, Fr Beaumont's point serves to alert us to the fact that Newman had a life of Christian faith before his so-called conversion aged forty-four. I think a disservice is done to the Anglican faith when Catholicism claims him solely as one of their own. The Catholic Church did not invent Newman!

A Student at Oxford University

Given John Henry Newman's remarkable intelligence, it came as no surprise when he received a scholarship to university at the age of sixteen. Newman enrolled in Trinity College, Oxford in 1817 and was a diligent student for whom there was great expectation of academic success. He was incredibly hardworking, so much so that his health suffered. He did not do well in his final exams in 1820 due to exhaustion brought on by overwork. There was an expectation among his peers and teachers that he would receive a double first-class honours, but he barely scraped through with a pass. However, on the terms of his scholarship he was allowed to continue and with his obvious academic pedigree he was elected to a fellowship at Oriel College, Oxford in 1822. In effect, this fellowship involved his being a tutor and mentor/monitor to other undergraduate students pursuing their degrees. It left Newman time to further his personal studies, as well as exposing him to the benefits of living in an academic environment steeped in tradition and culture. One might say he was in his element and that it was at this time that the 'scholar' Newman really began to emerge.

The Early Church Fathers

In the academic world that Newman now thrived in, he became more and more immersed in the writings of the early Church. He had a radical desire and hunger to return to the roots, to revisit the infancy of the faith and see how that faith was received and passed on. He wished, as a student, to come as close as humanly possible to the source of faith.

He read voraciously from the early Fathers of the Church. According to his biographer Maisie Ward, he 'lived and moved more among the early Fathers than among his living friends, close as they were to him.'[3] Former Maynooth professor Dr Tom Norris highlights just how influential they were when he writes: 'Newman, in fact, wrote in the style of the Fathers, imitating his chosen models, Athanasius, Augustine and Gregory Nazianzen.'[4]

This immersion in the writings of the early Church fathers gave Newman a fresh insight into pre-Reformation thought and a sense of the unity of the Church bound together by the strong threads of scripture, creed and tradition. Gradually, over the ensuing decades as he studied the early Church Fathers, he discovered the universal dimension of the Church, or as he himself called it, the sense of the 'Catholic'. He discovered the importance of what he termed the 'apostolicity' of the Church, that it is rooted in an unbroken tradition going back to the time of the Apostles themselves. The Church of England, in his view, had lost the sense of 'Catholicity' and 'apostolicity' and had become a more national Church that considered itself 'Protestant'. Newman was a son of this Church that King Henry VIII had established after breaking with Rome and aligning with the Protestant Church of Luther. Newman felt that the Church of England was at a great loss because of its rejection of much of the Catholic tradition. He was slowly beginning to feel not at home in this Church.

Call to Holy Orders and Pastoral Work

Newman did not leave Anglicanism until 1845. Far from being on overnight 'epiphany', Newman's path to joining the Roman Catholic Church was more an evolution in thought, prompted by a prolonged period of study and personal prayer. He had made a home for himself in the Church of England and answered a vocation to serve as a minister of that Church. While still teaching, he was ordained a deacon in 1824 and took holy orders in the Church of England soon afterwards. His first pastoral appointment was to the working-class parish of St Clement's in Oxford where he threw himself into his work with great zeal and with a deep-rooted concern for the pastoral needs of the poor. He was now a priest of the Church of England and happy to be one.

Preacher at St Mary's

He began his preaching life in St Mary's, the Oxford University Church. He soon became famous for his sermons, which captivated townspeople, students and fellows of the university alike. Many of his early sermons from this time explored the topics of social justice – which would clearly have resonated with those parishioners who were struggling with poverty – as well as more abstract themes of a theological and spiritual nature.

His sermons were usually over thirty minutes in length. He read from a preprepared text without raising his eyes towards the congregation and spoke in what observers described as a 'musical voice' with long pauses between sentences. By today's standards, Newman wasn't a great communicator and by those same standards it looks like he did everything that would empty a church on a Sunday today. Despite that, he still drew large crowds, impressed by the content of the homilies as well as the charisma and genuine sincerity of the enlightened preacher.

Throughout this time, Newman worked harder than ever. He had a strong and rigid work ethic that pushed him to his limits. He once preached:

> You should do a good deal of hard work in your generation, and prosecute many useful labours, and effect a number of religious purposes, and send many souls to heaven, and take men by surprise, how much you were really doing, when they happened to come near enough to see it.[5]

Inevitably, he would struggle with the strain of work. A series of personal difficulties in 1827 and 1828 weighed heavily on his spirit. He fell ill yet again due to overwork leading to a kind of nervous collapse, aggravated by the strain of worrying about the financial difficulties of his family. He was bereaved and deeply saddened by the death of his much-loved younger sister, Mary, who passed away after a brief illness, the details of which are unknown. John Henry thought of her often, especially on her anniversary, right throughout his long life. In one of his letters, written just ten months after Mary died, Newman felt her presence and heard her voice constantly. He told his sister Harriet in that letter that he felt blessed by this comfort, but he had still felt grief and regret: 'All I lament is, that I do not think that she ever knew how much I loved her.'[6]

Grief, physical exhaustion and anxiety necessitated his taking time off from teaching duties. In typical fashion, however, rather than take the opportunity to recuperate, he used this period to delve further into the literature of the early Church. His work ethic transpired to be both his ailment and his salvation. During this time, he produced a work called *The Arians of the Fourth Century* (1833). This was an exploration of the controversy surrounding the so-called 'Arian heresy' – the idea that Jesus is an exemplary man, but *not* God. Newman's book shows how such ideas nearly destroyed the Church in the fourth and fifth centuries. Some see Newman's thinking as a warning that Arianism lies behind the rise of secularism in today's world. His work was well received, and it led him to write *An Essay on the Development of Christian Doctrine*, which is regarded as the work that marked his entry into the Catholic Church.

Lead Kindly Light

I am aware that, so far, I have presented John Henry Newman as being preoccupied with study and the pursuit of matters wholly esoteric, but his writing did find a wide audience at the time. In 1833, Newman was spending some leisure time in Sicily where he contracted typhoid and nearly died. Eventually he recovered and, on 13 June, secured passage aboard an orange boat sailing to Marseilles, the first leg of his journey back to England; however, the boat was becalmed for a week and did not arrive at its destination until 27 June. Newman often wrote poetry to clarify his thoughts and on 16 June he penned 'The Pillar of the Cloud', which became better known as the hymn, 'Lead Kindly Light'. It is an expression of thanksgiving and trust born out of his near-death experience.

Lead, kindly light, amid the encircling gloom
Lead Thou me on!
The night is dark, and I am far from home –
Lead Thou me on!
Keep Thou my feet; I do not ask to see
The distant scene – one step enough for me.

I was not ever thus, nor pray'd that Thou
Shouldst lead me on.
I loved to choose and see my path; but now
Lead thou me on!
I loved the garish day, and, spite of fears,
Pride ruled my will; remember not past years.

So long Thy power hath blest me, sure it still
Will lead me on.
O'er moor and fen, o'er crag and torrent, till
The night is gone:
And with the morn those angel faces smile
Which I have loved long since, and lost awhile.

The Oxford Movement

With a new-found optimism following his serious illness, Newman was convinced that he needed to move on with his life back in Oxford. He states in *Autobiographical Writings,* 'God has still work for me to do.' He never lost hope and battled on despite any setback that came his way. In a sense, one might suggest that he thrived on setbacks and hardships as he viewed them as the building blocks of holiness. This approach he learned at an early age from the writing of the Rev. Thomas Scott, who taught holiness as the goal of Christian living: 'Holiness rather than peace.' This became Newman's first motto.

Upon his return to England, he and his Anglican colleagues began a movement that was to become known as the Oxford or Tractarian Movement, an ongoing project geared towards a spiritual and intellectual renewal of the Church of England. One of the main aims of the Oxford Movement was to reawaken in the Church of England a consciousness of its identity and mission through exploration of its neglected liturgical and spiritual heritage. There was then a sense in the Church of England of a 'spiritual torpor' and 'doctrinal indifference', partly stemming from the appointment of bishops by the government, along with an adherence to state policies and a preoccupation with status in society.

Parochial and Plain Sermons

As part of this new movement's momentum for renewal in the Church, Newman began to compile a collection of his sermons, *Parochial and Plain Sermons*, which has now become a classic of Christian spirituality. In these reflections we see an emphasis on the incarnation, the Resurrection, the indwelling of the Holy Spirit, the mystery of Christian revelation and the call to holiness – all doctrines pertinent to the Roman Catholic faith but that the Church of England sometimes treated with indifference.

Tracts for the Times

In addition to Newman's Sunday sermons, a series of pamphlets called *Tracts for the Times* was also issued in a bid to promote the work of the Oxford Movement. Ninety tracts were to be published anonymously, with Newman being the author of about one third of them. In essence, these tracts were impassioned appeals to the clergy and leadership of the Church of England to reform their Church and to find more meaning in the message of Christ – to look inwardly and seek renewal.

Newman describes his state of mind during his involvement with the Oxford Movement as one of 'confidence, of firmness, of zeal for the cause, of aggressiveness, of fierceness and of sport'.[7] He was no longer the shy, retiring fellow of Oriel of a few years previous; instead, Newman was bounding with energy and passion for his work. His students, inspired by his contagious enthusiasm, were often heard uttering the slogan: '*Credo in Newmanum!*' Newman was finding his feet as he passionately pleaded for the betterment of the Church of England, but challenges lay ahead.

Via Media

Newman was anxious in the *Tracts* to show that the Anglican position was occupying the *via media*, a mid-way between the extremes of Protestantism and Catholicism. He was more than content with this middle ground as he saw it as more credible than that of the Roman Catholic Church, which he had been brought up to distrust. One senses that Newman felt this (middle) ground begin to shift beneath his feet. His ongoing study of the Church Fathers brought him to draw the conclusion that, in fact, it was the Catholic Church that rightly occupied the *via media*. This realisation led to a major crisis for him. He was the leading light in the Oxford Movement's wish to renew the Church of England, but the kindly light of truth was leading him away from the Movement. He was beginning to feel like a stranger in his home church. His gradual move towards Catholicism had begun and was given an even stronger impetus when, in 1841, Newman published the ninetieth highly contentious tract, which demonstrated how the thirty-nine articles of the Anglican Church were 'patient of a Catholic interpretation'. That same year he returned to his study of patristics and this further consolidated his position.

Gradually, through his reflection and study of the early Church, Newman began to feel that it was the Church of England that was in a state of schism and the Roman Catholic Church that was actually 'the Church of the Apostles'. One can only imagine the inner turmoil this realisation must have caused him and, beyond that, how his peers would have reacted if he was to act upon his new-found set of beliefs.

Littlemore

Since 1840 Newman had been planning to found a type of monastic or religious community (which was not part of the tradition of the Church of England) and in 1842 he moved into a series of cottages, in a place called Littlemore, about two miles from Oxford where he had built a church and a school for the villagers. Locals called the house 'the Monastery' or, more commonly, 'the College'. The place has been restored and it can be visited today in the original 'joyful simplicity' style of the 1840s. Newman's life there became one of prayer, fasting and reflection and, while there, he became more and more convinced that the Roman Catholic Church had, in fact, remained faithful to what he and his fellow Tractarians termed the 'ethos of Primitive Christianity'.

The Parting of Friends

He demonstrated great courage, but felt he had no choice but to take the step to conversion. His ideas on the development of doctrine, and his nuanced ideas on scripture, creeds and tradition were groundbreaking in the area of theology and faith. Newman's life had become a beacon of hope in the realm of ecumenism and remains so today.

In 1843, Newman preached the last of his Oxford University Sermons, 'The Theory of the Developments in Religious Doctrine'. In September of that year he resigned as vicar of St Mary's and preached his last sermon as an Anglican, 'The Parting of Friends'. In 1844, he revealed to friends that he was on the verge of joining the Roman Catholic Church. The dark night of the soul was finally over and the day of his conversion came; it happened in a short moment of time. He resigned his fellowship of Oriel College and on 9 October 1845, without fanfare, Newman was received into the Roman Catholic Church by Fr Dominic Barberi, an Italian Passionist priest who was passing through Oxford.

One can only imagine the effect such a decision had on Newman as it would have meant cutting himself off from almost everyone he would have known. His parents were by then deceased and he was to a great extent alienated from the rest of his family. He wrote a moving letter to his sister Jemima. His two sisters had married two brothers and even they had minimal contact with him at this juncture. Of his two brothers, Frank was successful in life and Charles became a drifter; both of them became atheists. The Roman Catholic faith was widely mistrusted and any Anglican who embraced it was in effect ostracising themselves from those they knew.

1. 'History of My Religious Opinions', *Apologia Pro Vita Sua*.
2. Beaumont, *Blessed John Henry Newman: Theologian and Spiritual Guide for Our Times*, p. 2.
3. M. Ward (ed.), *Apologia Pro Vita Sua*.
4. Norris, *Cardinal Newman for Today*, p. 14.
5. Sermon 12, part 2 on St Philip Neri, *Sermons Preached on Various Occasions*.
6. *Letters and Diaries*, vol. ii, 'Tutor at Oriel'.
7. Referenced in Trevor, *Newman: The Pillar of the Cloud*, p. 45.

PART TWO

The Post-Conversion Years 1845–1890

Newman the Oratorian

Newman travelled to Rome in 1846 to study for the Catholic priesthood. While there, he found himself attracted to the Oratory – from the Latin word *orare*, meaning 'to pray' – of St Philip Neri, founded by that saint in the sixteenth century. He availed of the opportunity to join the Oratory and was ordained a priest in 1847. The Oratory, as founded by Neri, offered a more simplified view of religious communal living. It is a pontifical society of Catholic priests and lay-brothers who live in community but do not take formal religious vows. I imagine that Newman was attracted to the Oratorian style because in many ways it mirrored the concept he had created in Littlemore. The Oratory style of living allowed for great personal independence and this appealed to Newman who would have appreciated the individual freedom that life offered, as opposed to a more highly regulated religious institute or order.

It might seem unusual that Newman was attracted to Neri as they were so different in temperament. Neri was reputed to have been joyful and somewhat eccentric, whereas Newman was serious, highbrow, conventional, austere and reserved. On closer examination, however, the similarities between them are greater than their differences. They were both self-consciously reformers, setting out to renew the life of the Church through a return to the sources of the faith. Each in his private life emphasised the Church's teaching and the central place of prayer. Both combined the contemplative life with active pastoral concern. Equally, they displayed a positive attitude towards contemporary culture and sought to transform it from within.

Bear in mind that Newman was only a short time a Catholic and may have been suffering from the first effects of spiritual and intellectual 'jet lag'. It was not an easy transition and, before long, this intellectual giant felt cramped by the general mediocrity of Roman intellectual life. One example of this was his being presented with compilations of extracts from the Early Church Fathers' work – this to a man who had immersed himself for years in their original and entire oeuvre!

An English Oratory

Having done an Oratorian novitiate in Rome, Newman was happy to return home. He came back to England with a mission to found, in 1848, the first Oratorian community in Birmingham. There Newman welcomed the opportunity to combine ordinary pastoral work with academic and scholarly work. In 1849, a second oratory was founded in London, thereby adding the renewal of interest in the Oratorians and, because of that, Newman is to this day regarded as a second 'founder' of the Oratory. It seemed that Newman had found a role in the Catholic Church that suited his spirituality, personality and studious nature.

Later in life, in a bid to counter gossip that he felt unwelcome in the Catholic Church and was unhappy there, Newman spoke directly of 'a perfect peace and contentment' he found in the Catholic Church. He likened it to a boat arriving in port following a voyage on rough seas. Returning from Rome in 1848, the time ahead promised an abundance of that perfect peace and contentment in his native England.

He may never have thought that, just as in the fifth century when a cry of 'come and walk among us' went out to another British man (St Patrick), in 1851 a not dissimilar cry would wind its way across the Irish sea to him in the form of a request from the Irish bishops to come and found a Catholic university in Dublin.

An Irish Interlude 1851–1858

In 1851, at the request of Monsignor Cullen (who a year later became the Archbishop of Dublin), Newman was asked to give a series of lectures in Dublin designed to rally support for setting up a Catholic university in the city. These lectures later became incorporated into a classic volume called *The Idea of a University*, which is much quoted even today in education circles. Newman promoted the value of 'liberal education' as opposed to all forms of utilitarianism, which sees value only in 'useful' knowledge that might be put to practical effect. His notion of a liberal education is explained in his expressed aim of a university operating not merely to impart knowledge to students, but in affording students the opportunity to grasp the relationship between the different 'sciences' of disciplines. This notion of the coherence or interconnectedness of things is a hallmark of Newman's thinking.

Founding of the Catholic University

Following the series of lectures, Newman was invited to come to Ireland and set up the Catholic University of Ireland (the precursor to University College Dublin) at 86 St Stephen's Green. Without state funding and with the Irish bishops – in the words of Newman himself – being 'divided as to its expediency', he knew his mission was going to be a difficult one.

For those years Newman was combining the two position of being superior of the Birmingham Oratory and rector of the Catholic University, and he would make the arduous and wearisome journey across the Irish Sea by boat over fifty times during those years. During that same period he underwent one of the biggest ordeals of his life, the so-called 'Achilli affair'. In one of his books he had exposed the unsavoury career of a former Italian priest, Giacinto Achilli. Following this, Newman was charged with criminal libel and he had a huge battle on his hands to defend this unjust charge. This took a huge toll on him personally, but despite this Newman was very grateful for the moral and financial support he received from many sources to defend this case, which turned out to be a pyrrhic victory for Achilli, whose reputation was ultimately ruined.

Contentment to be in Ireland

Newman spoke often of his great love for Ireland and the Irish people. He was delighted with the warmth of welcome he received. He spoke of being 'killed with kindness'. Many of his experiences in Ireland amused him greatly and some of his funniest letters were written while there.

He wrote of the experience he had from a most kindly, but strong-willed housekeeper at one stage:

> When I got here, I found that the housekeeper, who would not let any other of the servants do it, had arranged not only my clothes, but all my papers for me. I had put my letters in various compartments according to my relations towards them – and my Discourse papers, according as I had done with them or not. She had mixed every thing, laying them most neatly according to their size. To this moment I have not had the courage to attempt to set them right – and one bit, which was to have come in, I have from despair not even looked for. And so of my linen; I had put the linen in wear separate from the linen in reserve. All was revolutionised. I

> could find nothing of any kind. Pencils, pens, penknife, toothbrush, boots … 'twas a new world – the only thing lef [sic], I suppose from a certain awe, was (woe's me) my discipline.[1]

Elsewhere Newman refers to meeting Archbishop John MacHale of Tuam who 'shook my hand with so violent a cordiality when I kissed his ring, as to punish my nose!'[2]

Newman did not conceal his sympathies with Irish nationalism. In that respect, years later Gerard Manley Hopkins, whom Newman received into the Catholic Church, was admonished by Newman for his excessive opposition to Irish nationalism, during his time as teacher of classics in Dublin.

'Baulks' Affecting Progress

So why, despite Newman's apparent happiness to be in Ireland and his love for the Irish people, did the experience sour to the point where Louis McRedmond refers to him as being 'thrown among strangers'? Newman's favourite word for obstacles and challenges (of which he had many in life) was a 'baulk'. Despite Newman's endeavours, the Irish University failed because of various 'baulks' and ultimately he must have been saddened that what he termed his 'campaign in Ireland' didn't bear more fruit.

Newman's own university background and experience was in sharp contrast to the more limited aspirations of the Irish bishops. The bishops of Ireland wanted an institution more like a seminary, with clergy in all the key positions and control over the curriculum. At that time, the bishops of Ireland had their hands full in building up parish structures and establishing a fuller spiritual life for Catholics throughout the country. Funding for the project was always going to be a challenge. Ireland was just recovering from the Great Famine and didn't have a sufficiently large and prosperous middle class that would be able to support such a university. The expected support for the project from England did not arrive, with few enough parents willing to send their children to study in the new college, despite the fact that there was no such facility at home. Despite his mild manner and the sophistication and gentle subtlety of his writing, Newman seemed to attract a number of powerful enemies, both within the Anglican and Catholic worlds. Moreover, as a man ahead of his time, his progressive ideas were not always embraced by his contemporaries and it would be almost a century after his death before his writings were fully embraced. Quite often he experienced considerable opposition to this work and ideas. Being of a sensitive nature, Newman took offence easily and suffered greatly because of this. McRedmond's intriguing summation of his Irish interlude as being 'thrown among strangers' may well hit the nail on the head and perhaps Newman did not really understand the Irish people as well as he thought.

Two Roaring Lions

The appointment of the first six professors and nine lecturers indicate some of the difficulties Newman encountered at that time. The list in question was sent to the four archbishops for approval. The two most influential were Paul Cullen of Dublin and John MacHale of Tuam. Both rarely agreed on anything! Cullen, being a former rector of the Irish College in Rome, was influential both with Rome and the British government. MacHale was an Irish nationalist and distrustful of both. He was dubbed the 'Lion of the West' because of his belligerent manner. Three of the archbishops approved the proposals, but not MacHale who wrote a curt letter to Newman complaining about a lack of consultation in drawing up the list and hinting that Cullen and Newman between them were trying to take over the university. Newman's reply was courteous, but firm and he sent a humorous account to his personal assistant Ambrose St John explaining what happened: 'The Lion, solus, has roared at me – and I have roared again – and the two roarings are done up in a letter sent to Dr Cullen at Rome.'

The University Years

Newman was rector of the new university from 1851 to 1858, overseeing the establishment of five faculties which were set up there: theology; law; medicine; philosophy and letters; and science. On 3 November 1854, the university opened its doors to a modest number of students, but with the hope of more to come.

University Church – St Stephen's Green

In 1856 a University Church was built and consecrated on St Stephen's Green at Newman's own expense and was adorned by Irish craftsmen in the Byzantine style. It is thought that Newman had in mind to one day found an oratory in Dublin and that this church could be part of its care. It is one of the most visited places in Dublin today. It was recently renovated and is a most popular inner-city venue for regular worship and for those seeking respite from the hustle and bustle of the busy city. To this day, it serves a purpose that Newman would be proud of.

A Final Word on the University Project

To summarise then, Newman's involvement with the Irish Catholic University marked some of the most turbulent years of his life as a new Catholic. It is only right to acknowledge that he did not seem to relate well to the Irish hierarchy; nor they to him. It would not be unkind either to suggest that the experience of the university project for both parties was a bit like the curate's egg – bad, but good in spots. One of its most positive legacies is that it gave to the English language one of its classic pieces of prose, Newman's *The Idea of a University*; it was also the springboard for the founding of University College Dublin (UCD) and it gave Dublin the beautiful University Church.

There were those who regarded the Catholic University of Ireland as a failure, with Newman being treated badly, 'thrown among strangers' and 'rejected by the Irish'. He wrote in a letter to Edward Caswal in 1854, 'No one knows but myself the desolateness in leaving Birmingham, and being thrown among strangers – I trust it will be taken as my penance, and be of eternal good to me.'[3] However, it was a heroic attempt to ensure equality of educational opportunity, a struggle which continued until the establishment of the National University of Ireland in 1908.

A Killaloe Diocesan Link to Newman

I note, with interest, that Eugene O'Curry was appointed professor of Irish history and archaeology at the new university in 1851. He was a Clare man from Doonaha, near Carrigaholt. O'Curry was previously elected a member of the Royal Irish Academy in 1851.

Another interesting Killaloe link is that of Rev. Michael Flannery, of Killaloe diocese. There is reference in the Killaloe diocesan archives to Michael Flannery visiting Newman in the Oratory in Birmingham in 1849. In 1854 Archbishop Cullen appointed Flannery dean of the Catholic University. Upon Flannery's consecration as bishop of Killaloe in 1861 he was presented with a crozier and this crozier is now on loan from the Diocese of Killaloe to Clare Museum in Ennis, Co. Clare where it is on public display. The origin of the crozier is identified by an inscription on a 25 mm wide band of gold on the wooden staff, which reads:

> Presented to The Right Revd Doctor Flannery Lord Bishop of Killaloe by The Rectors & Professors of The Catholic University of Ireland, 1861.

While on the subject, I might be permitted to submit my own modest personal Killaloe link to Newman. In 1992 I submitted a thesis on Newman as part of my studies for a licentiate in sacred theology (STL). My subject was 'John Henry Newman: How Dependent are Catholics on Scripture for their Creed?' At that time my preoccupation was with Newman, but his past and certainly my future connection with Killaloe Diocese never entered my head. I can only wonder at divine providence, or as Newman himself once said, 'Catholicism is a deep matter – you cannot take it up in a teacup.'

Influence of Dr Russell of St Patrick's College, Maynooth on Newman

Having read *Tract 90* a number of years earlier, a young Maynooth professor, Dr Charles William Russell, wrote to Newman to deplore his misrepresentation of the Catholic doctrine of transubstantiation. A correspondence began that became an important influence in Newman's conversion. In particular, Russell quelled Newman's fears regarding supposed excessive devotion to Our Lady. He convinced him that like other Catholic doctrines they were legitimate developments rather than the corruption of 'primitive principles'. In the *Apologia*, Newman says of Russell: 'He had perhaps, more to do with my conversion than anyone else.'[4]

A Newman–Daniel O'Connell link with the Irish College in Rome

A further interesting link, of sorts with Co. Clare and the new saint is a Newman–Daniel O'Connell link in the Irish College in Rome. There is a striking marble monument to Daniel O'Connell in the loggia of the Irish College in Rome. It provides a link of sorts between Newman, O'Connell (member of parliament for Co. Clare) and Co. Clare. The monument, reputed to contain the urn with the heart of O'Connell (which mysteriously went missing!), was removed from the Church of St Agatha dei Gothi to the Irish College in 1927. It represents O'Connell at the bar of the House of Commons refusing to take the anti-Catholic oath, reputedly with the words: 'I at once reject this declaration, part of it I believe to be untrue, and the rest I know to be false.' The inscription on the monument reads:

> This monument contains the heart of O'Connell, who dying at Genoa on his way to the eternal city, bequeathed his soul to God, his body to Ireland, and his heart to Rome.

The text on the monument was composed by Newman.

St Isidore's College, Rome Link with Newman

Another interesting Irish link with Newman is that of St Isidore's in Rome. Saint Isidore's College, founded by Luke Wadding, was, until recently, the house of formation for Irish Franciscan theology students. Almost all Irish Franciscans studied there. Opposite the altar of St Francis is a recumbent effigy of Octavia Catherine Bryan, an eighteen-year-old Irish girl who caught a fever and died during a visit to Rome in 1846, the very day she was due to get married. She was the daughter of Colonel George Bryan, prominent in the Catholic Emancipation Movement. John Henry Newman, the future cardinal, but then a deacon studying in Rome as a convert from Anglicanism, was asked to preach his first sermon as a Catholic at the funeral of Colonel Bryan's daughter. He records the event in his diary.

1. Quoted in Sugg, *John Henry Newman*, p. 29.
2. Quoted in McRedmond, *Thrown Among Strangers*, p. 129.
3. Letter to Edward Caswell, *Letters and Diaries*.
4. Quoted in Ker, *John Henry Newman: A Biography*, p. 254.

PART THREE

Snatches of Newman

I am devoting this section to a personal selection of what I call 'snatches of Newman'. In effect, I am dipping into various pools of Newman's work and life that appeal to me and I hope will add to your appreciation and knowledge of the man.

But first, let me say this: reader, you may be weary. Newman's writing can be tiresome at times and I recommend the best way to approach his work is by casually dipping into any of his original writings you may have at your disposal. Read just a little of anything by Newman and ponder his use of the English language and allow his message to sink gently into your consciousness. Newman had his sudden religious awakening as a young child, but the reader of Newman has need of a gradual awakening to Newman. Dip into Newman's work and persevere. This reminds me that he wrote a prayer for perseverance. We could probably do with reciting it now. Here it is:

Prayer for Perseverance
May Christ support us all the day long
Till shades lengthen
And the evening comes
And the busy world is hushed
And a fever of life is over

And our work is done.
Then in his mercy
May he give us a safe lodging,
A holy rest
And peace at last.
Amen.

Consulting the Faithful

The role of the laity is an important topic in today's Church. Newman's acknowledgement of the role of the laity in the Church is generally regarded as a milestone in his thought.

In 1859, Newman was asked by the English bishops to become editor of a Catholic publication called *The Rambler*, which had fallen foul of the authorities because of its liberal views. Newman willingly took it on, but it was not long before further controversy ensued, and things went from bad to worse. The controversy arose in relation to the involvement of the state in education. Newman, in 1859, put together an important and far-reaching work called *On Consulting the Faithful in Matters of Doctrine*. In that important work he attempts to justify a fuller participation of the laity in the life of the wider Church.

Lay participation, as espoused by Newman, was not welcomed by many churchmen. An example of an extreme reaction is contained in a letter from Mgr George Talbot to Mgr Henry Manning, which asks:

> What is the province of the laity? To hunt, to shoot, to entertain. These matters they understand, but to meddle with ecclesiastical matters they have no right at all ... Dr Newman is the most dangerous man in England ...[1]

Poor Newman. The sheen was beginning to wear off his conversion and he began to be an object of profound suspicion, not only for those he had just abandoned in the Church of England, but even more so for the authorities of Rome he had recently embraced; this was to be the case for the next number of years until he got an opportunity to defend himself.

I cannot help but feel that despite his acute sensitivity to the unfair criticism that he received, Newman drew on his own inner strengths and humbly accepted his lot. After all, this was the man who said of possible sainthood, 'It is enough for me to black the saints' shoes – if St Philip uses blacking, in heaven.'[2] These words echo the humility of John the Baptist who said of Christ: 'The straps of [his] sandals I am not worthy to tie' (Lk 3:16).

Another Low Point

In 1863 his morale reached an all-time low and this is recorded in his private journal:

> O how forlorn and dreary has been my course since I have been a Catholic! Here has been the contrast – as a Protestant, I felt my religion dreary, but not my life – but, as a Catholic, my life dreary, not my religion.[3]

This is a classic example of a giant mood swing – that between life lived under two religions. Honestly, which do you think is preferable, a dreary life or a dreary religion?

The move from Anglicanism to Catholicism and the *Rambler* affair had taken its toll on Newman and he was at a low ebb. Towards the end of 1863 and into 1864, he attempted to hazard a response to some critics. To defend his personal integrity and elaborate on his conversion, he published a series of articles that were more theological than spiritual. They became an instant bestseller when put together under the title of the *Apologia Pro Vita Sua*.

The *Apologia* is generally accepted as being one of the greatest religious autobiographies of all time, often namechecked alongside St Augustine's *Confessions*. The favourable reception of the *Apologia* gave Newman a great boost to his confidence and made him financially secure. It paved the way for greater acceptance among many previously skeptical Catholics, as well as rehabilitating him in English public opinion.

The Question of Authority and Papal Infallibility

Even though Newman was invited by some bishops to accompany them in the role of *peritus* or theological expert to the first Vatican Council, he declined to go on the grounds that he was too old for it. He did, however, follow the debates on papal infallibility with great interest. His position on the issue was balanced and nuanced. He believed personally in it, but as a 'theological opinion' and not as a dogma to be held by all.

For Newman, there was an important distinction between 'active infallibility' which belonged to the pope alone and 'passive infallibility' invested in the Church as a whole and manifested in *sensus fidelium*. He was opposed to a solemn dogmatic definition and feared the effect on non-Catholic opinion as a result of the behaviour of extremists wishing to inflate the power of the papacy. In the end he was happy with the moderation in the terms of the definition.

Conscience

According to Pope Emeritus Benedict, no Christian thinker since St Augustine so enriched our thinking on personal conscience as Newman. The modern thinking on conscience, even among many Catholics, is that conscience is a purely subjective and autonomous phenomenon, the simple expression of our authentic 'self'. In the place of this secularised concept, Newman explains and defends the traditional concept of conscience as the 'voice' of God within us.

Newman's concept and definition of conscience is often misunderstood and quoted out of context. On the one hand, in his famous letter to the Duke of Norfolk on the subject, he describes conscience as the 'aboriginal Vicar of Christ'. Also, in a celebrated passage in the same work he proposes, almost flippantly, a toast to conscience at the expense of the guidance our faith might give:

> I add one remark. Certainly, if I am obliged to bring religion into after-dinner toasts, (which indeed does not seem quite the thing) I shall drink to the pope, if you please – still, to conscience first, and to the pope afterwards.[4]

Newman was very clear that we will always need to have our consciences educated and enlightened, through prayer, serious reflection and attentiveness to the teaching of the magisterium.

Hymns and Poetry

Newman's prayers, poems and hymns have led many a person to pray well and often, or at least twice as St Augustine taught (*Qui cantat bene bis orat* – 'They who sing well pray twice'). Like St Augustine, Newman loved Gregorian and Ambrosian chant. Many of his own poetic works have been set to beautiful and haunting melodies. The well-known hymns 'Lead Kindly Light' and 'Praise to the Holiest in the Height' have been sung with great fervor and gusto at so many liturgical and faith gatherings for generations. The composer Edward Elgar brought to musical life Newman's profound meditation on purgatory, 'The Dream of Gerontius', which contains the hymn, 'Praise to the Holiest in the Heights' and 'Firmly I Believe and Truly'. A huge number of the hymns right throughout the Liturgy of the Hours or Divine Office are from the pen of Newman.

Grammar of Assent – The Nature of Belief

In 1870, Newman wrote what many see as one of his finest works, *An Essay in Aid of a Grammar of Assent*. They would claim that it is as important if not more so than his major works, the *Apologia*, *An Essay on the Development of Christian Doctrine* and the *Idea of a University*.

It was the culmination of a lifetime of reflection on faith and the means of acquiring faith. It also dealt with the relationship between faith and morality, and faith and spirituality. This tour de force took Newman the best part of twenty years to complete. It is perhaps his most difficult and complex work.

My introduction to Newman's *Grammar of Assent* was in my first year of theology in Maynooth seminary. Our professor was Fr Tom Corbett (a Killaloe priest now ministering in the diocese) who waxed lyrical on the work with great emphasis on the section dealing with the 'Introduction to Faith'.

In the book Newman explores how, in an increasingly de-Christianised society, the scientific standards for evidence, belief, faith and assent are too narrow to explain faith to the non-believer. On the one hand, faith is a legitimate product of rational human logic; but on the other it cannot judge or comprehend the validity or totality of where it comes from in the whole human or sensory experience. 'Logic is loose at both ends,' according to the Master. He argues that where formal logical inference is impossible, it is the culmination of probabilities that leads to certainty. Newman coined the famous phrase 'the illative sense' which works on the human being in an almost sensory or instinctive way that somehow eludes the grasp of formal logical analysis.

Cardinal Newman

In 1879, having been largely vindicated or rehabilitated in the eyes of both Anglicans and Catholics following the publication of the *Apologia* and in recognition of his outstanding achievements and good work, Pope Leo XIII appointed Newman a cardinal. Among the many tributes paid to him around this time was one sent by an Anglican friend who described him as 'the most loved man in England and see in him, on account of this love, a powerful force for unity between all Christians!'

Newman chose as his motto the words of St Francis of Sales, *cor ad cor loquitur*, which means 'heart speaks to heart'. It sums up for many the depth of Newman's love expressed in his deep personal heartfelt relationship with Christ. His life was always that great heart-to-heart conversation that is true prayer.

Newman's Many Gifts and Talents

One of Newman's biographers, Sheridan Gilley, described him as a 'master of musical English prose', as 'the prince of English autobiographers', as 'one of the liveliest letter writers of the Victorian era'.[5] As well as all his published work and private journals he maintained a voluminous correspondence and wrote in longhand until his hand ached under the strain.

I am reminded of the late Archbishop Joseph Cassidy who ordained me to priesthood when he spoke of the influence of his own schoolteacher parents on his becoming a teacher. In his own inimitable way Joe Cassidy wrote, 'I had chalk in my blood.' I like to think that Newman the prolific writer had ink in his veins.

The Fiction Author

Newman wrote fiction as well as academic studies. He wasn't a bestselling novelist, but his writing talent easily extended to creative work. In 1848 he wrote an autobiographical novel called *Loss and Gain*. This novel is full of humour and gently satirical. It counteracts the idea some have that Newman was a dry and humourless personality. *Callista*, written in 1855, is the story of a third-century martyr for the faith. It describes sufferings, torture and death with what was regarded as unusual honesty and frankness for the time.

He has written about the process of literally putting words onto paper:

> I write, I write again; I write a third time in the course of six months. Then I take the third: I literally fill the paper with corrections so that another person could not read it. I then write it out fair for the printer. I put it by, take it up, I begin to correct again … I cannot count how many times this process is repeated.[6]

Most professional writers will recognise the process of writing as described by Newman. It shows his tenacity and seriousness as to the act of writing, but it is not a process unique to him.

Some Traits and Characteristics

John Henry Newman by all accounts was a placid, gentle, noble, polite personality of a sensitive disposition, a man who perhaps took offence easily, as apparent from some of his interactions while in Ireland. In the prologue to Louis McRedmond's *Thrown Among Strangers* we see that he was frequently subjected to such indignities as 'raw' or 'underdone' mutton at Irish clerical tables, poor transport, bad weather and other general inconveniences. I am sure that these many minor inconveniences, when put together, are enough to try the patience of any saint.

His biographer Gilley described him as 'a literary workaholic'. It is claimed that he wrote standing up (pictures of some of his writing desks attest to this) to assist in concentration and that anything he wrote went through multiple revisions, with as many as five or six drafts for important letters or items for publication. While writing his *Apologia*, it was not uncommon for him to spend up to twenty-two hours a day working on his text and in just seven weeks he had a work of over five hundred pages completed to his satisfaction.

It became apparent during his time as rector of the Catholic University that he was a gifted manager and organiser. He applied himself to the many tasks associated with founding and establishing the University, hiring staff, working out practical details and editing two magazines during that time. This contradicts the view that Newman was remote and poor at day-to-day administration. No, from an early age he had assumed family responsibility and he continued throughout his life to show he was on top of practical affairs.

Ironically, health-wise he was delicate and frail, and did not enjoy the best of health, even though he lived into his ninetieth year. He was extremely diligent, rarely took time off and was hugely conscientious and meticulous in everything he did. As someone close to Newman observed:

> From his early days he had a deep desire to lead an ascetic life, sometimes to the detriment of

> his physical health. He was sparing on taking food, took little time on idle activities and was severely disciplined in his habits of work.

One description of him runs as follows: 'From his earliest days … reading the scripture, daily prayer, self-examination and later regular reception of Holy Communion.' This seems to sum up the daily roster of his existence. He puts it thus:

> It is the saying of holy men that, if we wish to be perfect, we have nothing more to do than to perform the ordinary duties of the day well. A short road to perfection – short, not because easy, but because pertinent and intelligible. There are no short ways to perfection, but there are sure ones.[7]

1. Cf. Ker, 'The Idea of the Laity', *John Henry Newman: A Biography*.
2. Letter to a Ms Munro, who had called him a saint. Quoted in Strange (ed.), *John Henry Newman: A Portrait in Letters*.
3. *Autobiographical Writings*, p. 254.
4. *Certain Difficulties Felt by Anglicans in Catholic Teaching*, vol. ii, p. 261.
5. Gilley, 'Introduction', *Newman and His Age*.
6. Letter to W.G. Ward quoted in Cornwell, *Newman's Unquiet Grave: The Reluctant Saint*, p. 9.
7. Quoted in Ker, *John Henry Newman: Meditations and Devotions*, p. 104.

PART FOUR

A Saint for Our Time

Piecing Together the Life of St John Henry Newman

Our saints don't have to be saints all their lives. Like any of us might do, they grow into sainthood. It seems reasonable that all who die and go to heaven are saints and remain anonymous to all but those who knew and loved them in life.

Might it not be fair then to ask, why do we need saints at all? I have stated at the outset that we need saints because their lives show us an example to follow in our own lives in order to guide us on the path to God. Fundamentally, men and women who are named or unnamed saints come from the normal ranks of humanity. Naturally, it follows that saints too have their flaws and sins like all of us. It can only be said of Christ that he and he alone was like us in all things, but sin. No saint is without his or her imperfections and so we might say that they are like us in all things, but perhaps better at some things. It seems to me that the gap between us and the saints is either a very narrow one or a gaping gulf.

People have favourites among the Church's family of saints. For one reason, or many reasons, we are drawn to a particular saint. You hear people say, 'My mother had a great devotion to St Gerard Majella', the patron saint of expectant mothers, and you can be certain that this is down to her seeking his prayerful intercession for a safe pregnancy. The fact is that we like saints, even though we may find at times that they are distant from us and that they are unfamiliar to us – reading about the lives of the saints is not as prevalent today as it was in the past for everyday followers of Christ. Reader, I would be happy that you have made a beginning in the practice of reading about saints if you have persevered to this point!

A few lines from Newman might be encouraging at this point; words that affirm our confidence in Jesus' help as we 'pilgrim' through life, with the help of the saints:

> O my Lord Jesus, low as I am in Your all-holy sight, I am strong in You, strong through Your Immaculate Mother, through Your saints and thus I can do much for the Church, for the world, for all I love.[1]

We have seen that Cardinal Newman was a scholar who was well acquainted with the saints – those great Mothers, Fathers and Doctors of the Church. He also knew that holiness was not merely a matter of great learning or academic study. Holiness is available to all with or without qualifications in learning.

Ian Ker, one of the great authorities on Newman, describes him as 'a genius who was at the same time one of the great masters of English prose and also one of those very few Christian thinkers who may be mentioned in the same breath as the Fathers of the Church.'[2]

He ranks as a saint with the great intellectual saints of the past such as the four women Doctors of the Church, Hildegard of Bingen, Catherine of Siena, Teresa of Ávila, Thérèse of Lisieux and male saint-Doctors such as Ambrose, Jerome, Augustine, Francis of Sales. A Doctor of the Church is an 'add-on' to the declaration of sainthood if he or she has made a great and significant contribution to the understanding of scripture and the development of doctrine. In the case of St John Henry Newman, I believe that his being declared a Doctor of the Church will happen in due course.

So why does it take years and even centuries to be declared a saint? No more than the development of doctrine, championed by Newman, the reality, impact and influence of the saint takes time to manifest. So convinced was St Bernard of Clairvaux of the saintliness of his friend St Malachy of Armagh that when the latter died St Bernard replaced the requiem Mass with the Mass of All Saints at his funeral. Saint Francis of Assisi was so extraordinary that after his death he was immediately proclaimed a saint, vox populi. In more recent times, Mother Teresa of Calcutta was declared a saint almost immediately after death, both by popular acclaim and officially, because of her example and huge impact. In Newman's case the impact of his far-reaching influence took some time to emerge, but in no way takes from his greatness as a saint for our time.

Sheridan Gilley's eminently readable biography captures a great sense of the person that Newman was. He says: 'He is, after Bunyan, at once the most profound and passionate of our religious pilgrims; and that must be the best excuse for retelling the story.' In describing Newman's lasting influence, Gilley says:

> His intellectual legacy is immense, and to Christians outside the Roman Catholic Church he stands as a sign of hope that there can be an answer to religious skepticism at the point of meeting between criticism and orthodoxy and ancient and modern; so there is no ultimate contradiction between new truth and the truth once delivered to the saints. That truth, he thought, is to be found through that growth in holiness which is the only evidence of life, when heart speaks to heart; and it is from the shadows and images of this world that mind and heart pass into truth.[3]

We cannot escape making the conclusion that Newman's contribution to scholarship with emphasis on his theological work and his work on education was the great decider in his being chosen as a saint for our time. His canonisation honours Newman's great mind and his use of it for the service of the Church and the enlightenment of all thinking people.

Newman, the Man!

Nowadays, we place a strong emphasis on understanding not only what a person thinks but what he/she feels or felt in the lived moments of life. I often wonder about Newman the man and the emotional side of his life. How did this cerebral individual handle the everyday patterns of behaviour common to all of us? In other words, I speak of him as a man and how his humanity is part of the makings of his sainthood.

Father Joseph Bacchus who lived in Newman's community during the last years of his life made this striking observation about him:

> [He] carried the art of being ordinary to perfection. He was singular in nothing. He took his food, his recreation, went about his ordinary duties, conversed without any mannerisms whatsoever. He had no foibles, no crotchets. The best testimony to this is the absence of good stories about him.[4]

I cannot but feel that there is something too akin to hagiography about that description. We sense an old man who is almost being over reverenced by linking his situation to the driving force of Christian virtue. If anything, the description reduces him to an ageing automaton.

I find more of the man in Newman's own words as he reflects on the struggles of humanity:

> By sinning, by suffering, by correcting ourselves, by improving, we advance to the truth by experience of error; we succeed through failures. We know not how to do right except by having done wrong. We call virtue a mean, that is, as considering it to lie between things that are wrong. We know what is right, not positively, but negatively; we do not see the truth at once and make toward it, but we fall upon and try error and find it is not the truth. We grope about by touch, not by sight, and so by a miserable experience exhaust the possible modes of acting till naught is left, but truth, remaining. Such is the process by which we succeed; we walk to heaven backwards; we drive our arrows at a mark and think him most skillful whose shortcomings are the least.[5]

He is immersed in the pilgrim journey to heaven, but his path is an earthly one and the journey to be made through the struggles and uplifts of life on the ground. One cannot but admire the depth of the line, 'We walk to heaven backward.' This grounds Newman in the mundane and is redolent of the discomforting 'smell of the sheep' line of Pope Francis, who is a great admirer of John Henry Newman.

An Apostle of Friendship

Newman has been described as an apostle of friendship. He valued day-to-day contact with those among whom he lived. He grieved for friendships lost at the time of his conversion. He kept up numerous friendships with men and women by means of his letter-writing.

His closest friend of many decades was fellow priest, Ambrose St John. The latter was a close friend, confidant, secretary and general minder of Newman. He smoothed the path for him through many of the minor tasks of life and thereby gave him more time to concentrate on his life's mission. St John predeceased Newman and Newman requested that when the time came he would be buried in the same grave as Fr Ambrose St John. This request has given rise to some speculation about Newman's sexuality; however, from his writings and commitment to celibacy from a young age, along with his reaffirmation of that in later years, this speculation seems unfounded. Through all his personal relationships, he embodied the Gospel of Jesus Christ and spread the faith to many other people and now to an entirely new generation.

Newman dealt with topics that were complex and at times highly esoteric. Yet he was capable of a very human outlook on life. He never wanted to be a monk locked away in a monastery using up reams of paper and writing in the margins of pages. He liked the social interaction with the world around him. I think he is best described as living and enjoying the physical world, while at the same time escaping for long periods to the cloistered world of his mind. He was a man with a foot in both worlds, but he was a man. I would like to borrow (as did Robert Bolt) Robert Whittington's description of St Thomas More and say that John Henry Newman was 'a man for all seasons'.

Ecumenical Influence

Being a convert from Anglicanism to Catholicism, his influence in terms of ecumenism is significant. Ecumenism has benefitted from Newman's concept of *via media*. In recent decades the various Christian traditions have advanced through, towards and beyond the *via media* to a clearer understanding, acceptance and respect for shared ground. Gone is the rancour and distrust caused by Newman's conversion, to be replaced with mutual trust between Anglicanism and Catholicism. Newman would be surprised but equally pleased by this sea change in ecumenical relations. Someone jokingly said that if he lived today, he wouldn't need to convert!

Newman did some service to both his home church and his adopted church. Owen Chadwick has said that Newman spent the first half of his life 'winding up the Church of England to its Catholic heritage' and that he spent the second half of his life 'winding down the Church of Rome'. That is, he sought to persuade one set of Church leaders not to push their Catholicity into fanaticism, or superstition, or irrationality, or rigid hierarchy. He appealed to the Church of England to keep their minds open to the old principles of primitive Catholic faith.

The Catholic Church benefitted from the scriptural tradition Newman carried with him and he was instrumental in the advance of historical method. Above all, he felt that he had little choice but to convert because Catholicism is a mystery of the spirit, too glorious and too profound for the tidiest minds to limit; and that faith in God is always more real and more certain than language which seeks to describe faith in God.

His canonisation is not a reward for, or recognition of his conversion. No, his influence on the movement for Church unity has contributed more to the makings of his sainthood.

Single-minded Determination

Newman may not have been too keen on collective thinking. Being a scholar, he tended to spend much time on his own. Scholarship made demands like reading, reflecting, praying, researching and thinking things through before putting pen to paper. One could describe him as being single-minded and in his opinion that 'living movements do not come of committees', a remark he made in the context of the publication of the *Tracts* and in his *Apologia*. This opinion may have influenced his refusal of an invitation to attend the First Vatican Council and more than likely he would have done the same if he were living at the time of the groundbreaking Second Vatican Council.

Far-reaching Influence on Vatican Councils

At the Second Vatican Council, Abbot Butler said that he felt that Newman's spirit was 'brooding over the council'. According to Ian Ker, Vatican II, which has been called 'Newman's Council', inaugurated not only extensive changes and reforms in the Roman Catholic Church but opened in effect a whole new era in Christian history. The almost revolutionary return by Catholic theology to its scriptural and patristic roots has invested Newman's own theology, which was so deeply, even exclusively, rooted in the Bible and the Fathers, with a wholly new importance and significance.

The Newman scholar Charles Stephen Dessain wrote:

> At the Second Vatican Council the tides of clericalism, over-centralism, creeping infallibility, narrow unhistorical theology and exaggerated Mariology were thrown back, while the things Newman stood for were brought forward – freedom, the supremacy of conscience, the Church as communion, the return to scripture and the fathers, the rightful place of the laity, work for unity, all the efforts to meet the needs of the age, and for the Church to take its place in the modern world.[6]

It is my belief that Newman is a saint today predominantly because of the influence his life's work and his exemplary living had on the Second Vatican Council. Pope John XXIII opened the windows to let air in and Newman's influence wafted in with that fresh air to ensure that for once a living movement did come of committees.

Last Years

When John Henry Newman returned to God on 11 August 1890 he had been a cardinal for eleven years. His final years were of relative contentment and free from controversies. These years were a time he continued to devote to praying, writing, corresponding and reflecting, along with leading his growing community and expanding school. His funeral Mass in Birmingham Oratory was filled with bishops, hundreds of Catholic and Anglican clergy, along with dignitaries, public figures and many past pupils. Over fifteen thousand people lined the route for the funeral cortège from the Oratory to Rednal where one of England's and the Church's greatest sons was laid to rest.

Remains

Newman's grave was opened on 2 October 2008, with the intention of moving any remains to a tomb inside Birmingham Oratory for their more convenient veneration as relics. However, his wooden coffin was found to have disintegrated and no bones were found.

Venerable

In 1991, Newman was proclaimed venerable by Pope John Paul II, after an examination of his life and work by the Congregation for the Causes of Saints.

Miracles

In 2000, Jack Sullivan, a man studying for the diaconate in Boston, USA was on the verge of paralysis and claimed to have been miraculously healed after praying to Newman. The miracle was investigated and confirmed by the Vatican. A second miracle, necessary for canonisation, was approved by the Vatican in November 2018. This miracle concerned the healing of Melissa Villalobos from Chicago. She and her unborn baby had a life-threatening illness and it is believed that through the intercession of Newman both she and her baby survived.

Beatification

Newman was beatified on 19 September 2010 by Pope Benedict XVI.

Canonisation

On 1 July 2019, with an affirmative vote the canonisation was authorised and the date for the canonisation ceremony was arranged for 13 October 2019.

1. Quoted in Velocci, *Prayer in Newman*, p. 33.
2. Ker, *The Genius of John Henry Newman*.
3. Gilley, *Newman and His Age*, p. 3.
4. Fr Joseph Bacchus quoted in Cunningham (ed.), *John Henry Newman: Heart Speaks to Heart: Selected Spiritual Writings*.
5. 'The State of Innocence', *Parochial and Plain Sermons*, vol. v.
6. Dessain, *John Henry Newman*, p. 169.

PART FIVE

Some Saintly Gems

'Cor ad cor loquitur'
('Heart speaks to heart')
– Cardinal's motto, chosen because Newman admired its use in St Francis of Sales' *Introduction to the Devout Life*

'Ex umbris et imaginibus in veritatem'
('From shadows and images into the truth')
– Epitaph

Saint John Henry Newman has made a lasting impact on my life and I am grateful for that; however, I am not alone when it comes to being influenced by Newman. Throughout his life, Newman influenced many people and this is borne out by the many testimonies published at the time of his death. Most people seem to have sensed the essence of the man that came across through knowing him in person as well as through his writings. The *Aberdeen Evening Express* had the following to say about him when he died:

> In the death of Cardinal Newman one of the most outstanding personalities of the century has passed away. By his writings, as much as by his severance from the Church of England, followed by a long and saintly life, Newman has

> exercised an influence on the religious life of the country that is well-nigh incalculable.[1]

The *Cork Examiner* reiterated this by saying: 'Cardinal Newman goes to his grave with the singular honour of being by all creeds and classes acknowledged as the just man made perfect.'[2] Such tributes help us to appreciate from our present day remove the impact Newman made on all walks of life. Unhesitatingly, they acknowledge him as having the makings of a saint, which a century or more later is finally coming to fruition.

The late Cardinal Cahal B. Daly, who was himself cast from a similar intellectual mould, also sensed the personality and humanity of Newman when he wrote:

> Newman is undeniably one of the great writers and the stylists of all time, an incomparable master of the English language, whether spoken or written; but also one in whose writings the man himself becomes present as a warm, sensitive, loving, and above all intensely human personality.[3]

The Church in the modern world owes much to Newman for the manner in which he thought about our Catholic faith and the expression of those thoughts in imaginative writings. Pope John XXIII's initiation of the Second Vatican Council was hailed as the opening of a window to bring fresh air into the

Church. Newman's work was airborne and entered through that window. Charles Stephen Dessain has said of Vatican II:

> … the things Newman stood for were brought forward – freedom, the supremacy of conscience, the Church as communion, the return to scripture and the fathers, the rightful place of the laity, work for unity, all the efforts to meet the needs of the age, and for the Church to take its place in the modern world.[4]

Reader, I write of Newman's impact as a preamble to offering you a few select pieces from his writings that I hope will act as a taster to encourage you to come back for more; I assure you there's no shortage. It is my wish that you will gain as much pleasure from reading some of Newman's work as I have done through the years. I hopc you move from dipping into Newman's works to delving deeper into them and be confident all the while that you will have his saintly guidance to ease your way to a better understanding of the truths of your faith.

Newman's work includes several hymns from the Divine Office for matins, lauds, prime, terse, sext, none, vespers and compline.

(*PPS – Parochial and Plain Sermons*)
(*MD – Meditations and Devotions*)
(*LD – Letters and Diaries*)

Prayer to Our Lady

May the Blessed Mary
Be your Protection and Comfort
This day and all days
Till she welcomes you
To the eternal Home
Above.

(*LD*)

Marian Prayer of Cardinal Newman

O Mother of Jesus, and my Mother, let me dwell with you, cling to you and love you with ever-increasing love. I promise the honour, love and trust of a child. Give me a mother's protection, for I need your watchful care. You know better than any other the thoughts and desires of the Sacred Heart. Keep constantly before my mind the same thoughts, the same desires, that my heart may be filled with zeal for the interests of the Sacred Heart of your Divine Son. Instil in me a love of all that is noble, that I may no longer be easily turned to selfishness.

Help me, dearest Mother, to acquire the virtues that God wants of me: to forget myself always, to work solely for him, without fear of sacrifice. I shall always rely on your help to be what Jesus wants me to be. I am his; I am yours, my good Mother! Give me each day your holy and maternal blessing until my last evening on earth, when your Immaculate Heart will present me to the Heart of Jesus in heaven, there to love and bless you and your divine Son for all eternity.

(*A John Henry Newman Prayer Book*)

Ave Maris Stella

Hail then, Star of the Sea, we joy in the recollection of thee. Pray for us ever at the throne of grace; plead our cause, pray with us, present our prayers to thy son and Lord – now and in the hour of death, Mary be thou our help.

(*A John Henry Newman Prayer Book*)

The Jesus Prayer (The Fragrance Prayer)

Dear Jesus, help me to spread
Your fragrance everywhere
Flood my soul with your
Spirit and Your life.
Penetrate and possess my whole
Being so utterly that all
My life may be only a
Radiance of yours.
Shine through me and be so in
Me that every soul I come
In contact with may feel
Your presence in my soul
Let them look up and see no
Longer me, but only Jesus. Amen.

(Source unknown)

The Pillar of Cloud (Lead Kindly Light)

Lead, kindly light, amid the encircling gloom.
Lead thou me on!
The night is dark, and I am far from home.
Lead thou me on!
Keep thou my feet; I do not ask to see
The distant scene, one step enough for me.

I was not ever thus, nor pray'd that thou
Should lead me on.
I loved to choose and see my path; but now
Lead though me on!
I loved the garish day, and, spite of fears,
Pride ruled my will; remember not past years.

So long thy power hath blest me, sure it's still
Will lead me on.
O'er moor and fen, o'er crag and torrent, till
The night is gone:
And with the morn those angel faces smile
Which I have loved long since, and lost a while.

(*Verses on Various Occasions*)

Prayer for Perseverance

May Christ support us all the day long
Till shades lengthen
And the evening comes
And the busy world is hushed
And a fever of life is over
And our work is done.
Then in his mercy
May give us the safe lodging
A holy rest
And peace at last.
Amen.

(*MD*)

Anima Christi Prayer

Soul of Christ, be my sanctification;
Body of Christ, be my salvation;
Blood of Christ, fill all my veins;
Water of Christ's side, wash out my stains;
Passion of Christ, my comfort be;
O good Jesus, listen to me;
In Thy wounds I fain would hide;
Ne'er to be parted from Thy side;
Guard me, should the foe assail me;
Call me when my life shall fail me;
Bid me come to Thee above,
With Thy saints to sing Thy love,
World without end.
Amen.

(*MD*)

A Prayer to Begin the Day

And grant that to thine honour, Lord,
Our daily toil may tend;
That we begin it at thy word,
And in thy favour end.

(*A John Henry Newman Prayer Book*)

Prayer for a Happy Death

Oh, my Lord and Saviour, support me in that hour in the strong arms of your sacraments, and by the fresh fragrance of your consolations. Let the absolving words be said over me, and the holy oil sign and seal me, and your own body be my food, and your blood my sprinkling; and let my sweet mother, Mary, breathe on me, and my angel whisper peace to me, and my glorious saints smile upon me; that in them all, and through them all, I may receive the gift of perseverance, and die, as I desire to live, in your faith, in your Church, in your service, and in your love. Amen.

(*MD*)

Illuminating Grace

You ask, what it is you need, besides eyes, in order to see the truths of revelation; I will tell you at once; you need light. Not the keenest eyes can see in the dark. Now, though your mind be the eye, the grace of God is the light; and you will as easily exercise your eyes in this sensitive world without the sun, as you will be able to exercise your mind in the spiritual world without a parallel gift from without. Now, you are born under a privation of this blessed spiritual light, and, while it remains, you will not, cannot, really see God. I do not say you will have no thought at all about God, nor be able to talk about him. True, but you will not be able to do more than reason about him. Your thoughts and your words will not get beyond a mere reasoning. I grant then what you claim; you claim to be able by your mental powers to reason about God; doubtless you can, but to infer a thing is not to see it in respect to the physical world, nor is it in the spiritual.

(*Discourses Addressed to Mixed Congregations*)

Prayer for the Light of Truth

O my God, I confess that thou canst enlighten my darkness. I confess that thou alone canst. I wish my darkness to be enlightened. I do not know whether thou wilt: but that thou canst and that I wish, are sufficient reasons for me to ask, what thou at least hast not forbidden my asking. I hereby promise that by your grace which I am asking, I will embrace whatever I at length feel certain is the truth, if ever I come to be certain. And by Your grace I will guard against all self-deceit which may lead me to take what nature would have, rather than what reason approves.

(*MD*)

O My Lord Jesus

O my Lord Jesus, low as I am in Your all-holy sight, I am strong in You, strong through Your Immaculate Mother, through Your saints and thus I can do much for the Church, for the world, for all I love.

(*MD*)

Litany of the Resurrection

Lord, have mercy. *Lord, have mercy.*
Christ, have mercy. *Christ, have mercy.*
Lord, have mercy. *Lord, have mercy.*
Christ, hear us. *Christ, graciously hear us.*

God the Father of Heaven, *have mercy on us.*
God the Son, Redeemer of the world, *have mercy on us.*
God the Holy Ghost, *have mercy on us.*
Holy Trinity, one God, *have mercy on us.*
Jesus, Redeemer of mankind, *have mercy on us.*
Jesus, Conqueror of sin and Satan, *have mercy on us.*
Jesus, triumphant over Death, *have mercy on us.*
Jesus, the Holy and the Just, *have mercy on us.*
Jesus, the Resurrection and the Life, *have mercy on us.*
Jesus, the Giver of grace, *have mercy on us.*
Jesus, the Judge of the world, *have mercy on us.*
Who didst lay down thy life for thy sheep, *have mercy on us.*
Who didst rise again the third day, *have mercy on us.*

Who didst manifest thyself to thy chosen, *have mercy on us.*
Visiting thy blessed Mother, *have mercy on us.*
Appearing to Magdalen while she wept, *have mercy on us.*
Sending thy angels to the holy women, *have mercy on us.*
Comforting the Eleven, *have mercy on us.*
Saying to them, Peace, *have mercy on us.*
Breathing on them the Holy Ghost, *have mercy on us.*
Confirming the faith of Thomas, *have mercy on us.*
Committing thy flock to Peter, *have mercy on us.*
Speaking of the Kingdom of God, *have mercy on us.*
We sinners, beseech thee, *hear us, have mercy on us.*
That we may walk in newness of life, *have mercy on us.*
We beseech Thee, *hear us.*
That we may advance in the knowledge of thee, *hear us.*
That we may grow in grace, *hear us.*
That we may ever have the bread of life, *hear us.*

That we may persevere unto the end, *hear us.*

That we may have confidence before thee at thy coming, *hear us.*

That we may behold thy face with joy, *hear us.*

That we may be placed at Thy right hand in the judgement, *hear us.*

That we may have our lot with the saints, *hear us.*

Lamb of God, who takest away the sins of the world,

Spare us, O Lord.

Lamb of God, who takest away the sins of the world,

Graciously hear us, O Lord.

Lamb of God, who takest away the sins of the world,

Have mercy on us.

Christ, hear us.

Christ, graciously hear us.

Lord, have mercy.

Christ, have mercy.

Lord, have mercy.

Christ is risen, Alleluia.
He is risen indeed, and hath appeared unto Simon, Alleluia.

Let us pray.

O God, who by thy only begotten son hast overcome death, and opened on us the way to eternal life, vouchsafe, we beseech thee, so to confirm us by thy grace, that we may in all things walk after the manner of those who have been redeemed from their sins, through the same Jesus Christ our Lord. – *Amen.*

(*MD*)

THE CHALLENGE OF LIVING THE CHRISTIAN LIFE

Vocation Prayer – The Mission of my Life

God has created me to do him some definite service. He has committed some work to me which he has not committed to another. I have my mission. I may never know it in this life, but I shall be told it in the next. I am a link in a chain, a bond of connection between persons. He has not created me for naught. I shall do good; I shall do his work. I shall be an angel of peace, a preacher of truth in my own place, while not intending it if I do but keep his commandments. Therefore, I will trust him, whatever I am, I can never be thrown away. If I am in sickness, my sickness may serve him, in perplexity, my perplexity may serve him. If I am in sorrow, my sorrow may serve him. He does nothing in vain. He knows what he is about. He may take away my friends. He may throw me among strangers. He may make me feel desolate, make my spirits sink, hide my future from me. Still, he knows what he is about.

(*MD*)

The Simple Path to Holiness

It is the saying of holy men that, if we wish to be perfect, we have nothing more to do than to perform the ordinary duties of the day well. A short road to perfection – short, not because easy, but because pertinent and intelligible. There are no short ways to perfection, but there are sure ones.

I think this is an instruction which may be of great practical use to persons like ourselves. It is easy to have vague ideas what perfection is, which serve well enough to talk about, when we do not intend to aim at it; but as soon as a person really desires and sets about seeking it himself, he is dissatisfied with anything but what is tangible and clear, and constitutes some sort of direction towards the practice of it.

We must bear in mind what is meant by perfection. It does not mean any extraordinary service, anything out of the way, or especially heroic – not all have the opportunity of heroic acts, of sufferings – but it means what the word perfection ordinarily means. By perfect we mean that which has no flaw in it, that which is complete, that which is consistent, that which is sound – we mean the opposite to imperfect. As we know well what imperfection in religious service means, we know by the contrast what is meant by perfection.

He, then, is perfect who does the work of the day perfectly, and we need not go beyond this to seek for perfection. You need not go out of the round of the day.

I insist on this because I think it will simplify our views, and fix our exertions on a definite aim.

If you ask me what you are to do in order to be perfect, I say, first: Do not lie in bed beyond the due time of rising; give your first thoughts to God; make a good visit to the Blessed Sacrament; say the Angelus devoutly; eat and drink to God's glory; say the Rosary well; be recollected; keep out bad thoughts; make your evening meditation well; examine yourself daily; go to bed in good time, and you are already perfect.

(*MD*)

God's Plan for Us

God has created all things for good; all things for their greatest good; everything for its own good. What is the good of one is not the good of another; what makes one man happy would make another unhappy. God has determined, unless I interfere with His plan, that I should reach that which will be my greatest happiness. He looks on me individually, He calls me by my name, He knows what I can do, what I can best be, what is my greatest happiness, and He means to give it me.

(*MD*)

Learning What is Right and Wrong from an Early Age

Boys do not fully know what is good and what is evil; they do wrong things at first almost innocently. Novelty hides vice from them; there is no one to warn them or give them rules; and they become slaves of sin, while they are learning what sin is.

(*Loss and Gain: The Story of a Convert*)

Analysis of Virtue

Virtue is its own reward, and brings with it the truest and highest pleasure; but if we cultivate it only for pleasure's sake, we are selfish, not religious, and will never gain the pleasure, because we can never have the virtue.

(*Sayings of Cardinal Newman*)

HYMNS AND DEVOTIONAL WORK FROM *THE DREAM OF GERONTIUS*

The musical composition The Dream of Gerontius *is a work for voices and orchestra composed by Edward Elgar in 1900 using the text of the poem by Newman. It relates the journey of a pious man's soul from his deathbed to his judgement before God and settling into purgatory.*

Praise to the Holiest in the Height

Praise to the holiest in the height,
And in the depth be praise;
In all his words most wonderful;
Most sure in all his ways!

O loving wisdom of our God!
When all was sin and shame,
A second Adam to the fight
And to the rescue came.

O wisest love! That flesh and blood
Which did in Adam fail,
Should strive afresh against their foe,
Should strive and should prevail.

And that a higher gift than grace
Should flesh and blood refine,
God's presence and his very self,
And essence all-divine.
O generous love! That he who smote

In man for man the foe,
The double agony in man
For man should undergo;

And in the garden secretly,
And on the cross on high,
Should teach his brethren and inspire
To suffer and to die.

Firmly I Believe and Truly

Firmly I believe and truly
God is three and God is one;
And I next acknowledge duly
Manhood taken by the Son.

And I trust and hope most fully
In that manhood crucified;
And each thought and deed unruly
Do to death, as he has died.

Simply to his grace and wholly
Light and life and strength belong,
And I love supremely, solely,
him the holy, him the strong.

And I hold in veneration,
For the love of him alone,
Holy Church as his creation,
And her teachings, as his own.
And I take with joy whatever

Now besets me, pain or fear,
And with a strong will I sever
All the ties which bind me here.

Adoration aye be given,
Wash and through the angelic host,
To the God of earth and heaven,
Father, Son and Holy Ghost.

Prayer for the Dying

Go forth, Christian soul, from this world
In the name of God the almighty Father, who created you,
In the name of Jesus Christ, the Son of the living God, who suffered for you,
In the name of the Holy Spirit, who was poured out upon you. Go forth, Christian soul.
May you live in peace this day,
may your home be with God in Sion,
with Mary the virgin Mother of God, with Joseph and all the angels and saints …
May you return to [your Creator] who formed you from the dust of the earth.
May holy Mary, the angels and all the saints come to meet you as you go forth from this life …
May you see your Redeemer face to face.

MISCELLANEOUS

On Prayer

Prayer is the language of heaven.

(*Prayer in Newman*)

Prayer is conversing with God.

(*PPS*)

Prayer is to spiritual life what the beating of the pulse and the drawing of the breath are to the life of the body.

(*PPS*)

Prayer is a 'heart to heart' conversation.

(*Prayer in Newman*)

Prayer, praise, thanksgiving, contemplation are the peculiar privilege and duty of a Christian.

(*PPS*)

As speech is the organ of human society, and the means of human civilization, so prayer is the instrument of divine fellowship and divine training.

(*PPS*)

He who does not pray does not claim his citizenship with heaven, but lives, though an heir of the kingdom, as if he were a child of earth.

(*PPS*)

My Lord, I offer thee myself in turn as a sacrifice of thanksgiving.

(*MD*)

Everything that one does honestly, sincerely, with prayer, with advice, must turn to good.

(*LD*)

No one has access to the almighty as his mother has.

(*MD*)

On Conscience

It is often said that second thoughts are best. So they are in matters of judgement but not in matters of conscience.

(*Letter to the Duke of Norfolk*)

Conscience is the aboriginal Vicar of Christ.

(*Letter to the Duke of Norfolk*)

I add one remark. Certainly, if I am obliged to bring religion into after-dinner toasts, (which indeed does not seem quite the thing) I shall drink – to the Pope, if you please – still, to Conscience first, and to the Pope afterwards.

(*Letter to the Duke of Norfolk*)

On Education

If then a practical end must be assigned to a university course, I say it is that of training good members of society ... It is the education which gives a man a clear, conscious view of their own opinions and judgements, a truth in developing them, an eloquence in expressing them, and a force in urging them. It teaches him to see things as they are, to go right to the point, to disentangle a skein of thought to detect what is sophistical and to discard what is irrelevant.

(*The Idea of a University*)

A university training is the great ordinary means to a great but ordinary end; it aims at raising the intellectual tone of society ... It is the education which gives a man a clear conscious view of his own opinions and judgements, a truth in developing them, an eloquence in expressing them and a force in urging them.

(*The Idea of a University*)

There is a knowledge worth possessing for what it is and not merely for what it does.

(*The Idea of a University*)

On Being a Gentleman

Hence it is that it is almost a definition of a gentleman to say that he is one who never inflicts pain. He is mainly occupied in merely removing the obstacles which hinder the free and unembarrassed action of those about him; and he concurs with their movements rather than take the initiative himself.

His benefits may be considered as parallel to what are called comforts or conveniences in arrangements of a personal nature; like an easy chair or a good fire, which do their part in dispelling cold and fatigue, though nature provides both means of rest and animal heat without them. The true gentleman in like manner carefully avoids whatever may cause a jar or a jolt in the minds of those with whom he is cast – all clashing of opinion, or collision of feeling, all restraint, or suspicion, or gloom, or resentment; his great concern being to make every one at his ease and at home. He has his eyes on all his company; he is tender towards the bashful, gentle towards the distant, and merciful towards the absurd; he can recollect to whom he is speaking; he guards against unseasonable allusions, or topics which may irritate; he is seldom prominent in conversation, and never wearisome. He makes light of favours while he does them, and seems to be receiving when he is conferring.

He never speaks of himself except when compelled, never defends himself by a mere retort; he has no ears for slander or gossip, is scrupulous in imputing motives to those who interfere with him, and interprets everything for the best. He is never mean or little in his disputes, never takes unfair advantage, never mistakes personalities or sharp saying for arguments, or insinuates evil which he dare not say out. From a long-sighted prudence, he observes the maxim of the ancient sage, that we should ever conduct ourselves towards our enemy as if he were one day to be our friend. He has too much good sense to be affronted at insults, he is too well employed to remember injuries, and too indolent to bear malice. He is patient, forbearing, and resigned, on philosophical principles; he submits to pain, because it is inevitable, to bereavement, because it is irreparable, and to death, because it is his destiny.

If he engages in controversy of any kind, his disciplined intellect preserves him from the blundering discourtesy of better, perhaps, but less educated minds; who, like blunt weapons, tear and hack instead of cutting clean, who mistake the point in argument, waste their strength on trifles, misconceive their adversary, and leave the question more involved than they find it. He may be right or wrong in his opinion, but he is too clear-headed to be unjust; he is as simple as he is forcible, and as brief as he is decisive. Nowhere shall we find greater candour, consideration, indulgence: he throws himself into the minds of his opponents, he accounts for their mistakes. He knows the weakness of human reason as well as its strength, its province and its limits.

(*The Idea of a University*)

On the Role of the Laity

What I desiderate [desire] in Catholics is the gift of bringing out what their religion is. I want a laity, not arrogant, not rash in speech, not disputatious, but men who know their religion, who enter into it, who know just where they stand, who know what they hold and what they do not, who know their creed so well that they can give an account of it, who know so much of history that they can defend it. I want an intelligent, well-instructed laity. I wish you to enlarge your knowledge, to cultivate your reason, to get an insight into the relation of truth to truth, to learn to view things as they are, to understand how faith and reason stand to each other, what are the bases and principles of Catholicism and where lies the main inconsistencies and absurdities of the Protestant theory. I have no apprehension you will be the worse Catholics for familiarity with these subjects, provided you cherish a vivid sense of God above and keep in mind that you have souls to be judged and saved. In all times the laity have been the measure of the Catholic spirit; they saved the Irish Church three centuries ago and they betrayed the Church in England. You ought to be able to bring out what you feel and what you mean, as well as to feel and mean it; to expose to the comprehension of others the fictions and fallacies of your opponents; to explain the charges brought against the Church, to the satisfaction, not, indeed, of bigots, but of men of sense, of whatever cast of opinion.

(*Lecture on 'The Present Position of Catholics' in England,* 1851)

On Certainty

If we insist on being as sure as is conceivable ... we must be content to creep along the ground, and never soar.

(*John Henry Newman: A Biography*)

On Love

Love is his bond, he knows no other fetter.
Asks not our all, but takes whatever we spare him.
Willing to draw us on from good to better,
As we can bear him.

(*Verses on Various Occasions*)

On the Clerical Life

Blessed John Henry Newman in 'Witnesses to the Resurrection' asked himself why did God use a few souls to begin and continue the work of the Church, and he answered in this way: 'I have already suggested, what is too obvious almost to insist upon, that in making a select few the ministers of his mercy to mankind at large, our Lord was but acting according to the general course of his providence. It is plain every great change is effected by the few, not by the many; by the resolute, undaunted, zealous few.'

(*PPS*)

On the Saints

In the schools of science, England has no name to rival Erigena in originality, or St Virgil in freedom of thought nor among its canonised women any saintly virgin to compare with St Bridget, nor although it has one hundred and fifty canonised saints in its calendar, can it pretend to equal that Irish multitude which the book of life alone is large enough to contain.

(*Historical Sketches*)

On Living Fully

Let us act on what we have, since we have not what we wish.

(*Discussions and Arguments on Various Subjects*)

We can believe what we choose. We are answerable for what we choose to believe.

(*Letter to Mrs William Froude*, 27 June 1848)

Nothing would be done at all if one waited until one could do it so well that no one could find fault with it.

(Quoted in *Developing the Leader Within You*)

Growth is the only evidence of life.

(*The Westminster Collection of Christian Quotations*)

Fear not that thy life shall come to an end, but rather that it shall never have a beginning.

(*Sayings of Cardinal Newman*)

If we are intended for great ends, we are called to great hazards.

(*Oxford University Sermons*)

On Evil

Humility, awareness of sinfulness – we advance towards God even by means of our mistakes and failures.

(*PPS*)

Evil has no substance of its own, but is only the defect, excess, perversion, or corruption of that which has substance.

(*On the Scope and Nature of a University Education*)

On Catholicism

From the age of fifteen, dogma has been the fundamental principle of my religion: I know no other religion; I cannot enter into the idea of any other sort of religion; religion, as a mere sentiment, is to me a dream and a mockery.

(*Apologia Pro Vita Sua*)

We must make up our minds to be ignorant of much, if we would know anything.

(*Discussions and Arguments on Various Subjects*)

To be detached is to be loosened from every tie which binds the soul to the earth …

(*Historical Sketches*)

… the human mind is made for truth …

(*The Grammar of Assent*)

Catholicism is a deep matter – you cannot take it up in a teacup.

(*Letter to J. Spencer Northcote,* 8 February 1846)

On the Parting of Friends

My sole ascertainable reason for moving is a feeling of indefinite risk to my soul in staying … shall one bear to live, where die one cannot!

(*Letter to John Keeble,* 21 November 1844)

On Change

… to live is to change, and to be perfect is to have changed often.

(*An Essay on the Development of Christian Doctrine*)

On the Spiritual Struggle

After the fever of life – after weariness, sickness, fightings and desponding languor and fretfulness, struggling and failing, struggling and succeeding – after all the changes and chances of this troubled and unhealthy state, at length comes death – at length the white throne of God – at length, the beatific vision.

(*Heart to Heart: A Cardinal Newman Prayer Book*)

On the Role of a Priest

The duty of a priest is to remind people that 'life is short, death is certain, eternity long'.

(*PPS*)

GENERAL QUOTATIONS ATTRIBUTED TO NEWMAN

In his introduction to Meditations and Devotions, *Ian Ker writes that 'Newman was accustomed to note down, in the roughest way, any thought that particularly struck him while meditating, that he might reflect upon it during the day or pursue it in the future; and this he was led on to enlarge such thoughts, and write out the notes and re-write them carefully (for he always, he said, could meditate best with a pen in his hand). With "one or two exceptions" all the heading of various "subjects", as well as "their parts and chapters", were the work of the author, although, "their order evidently had not always been fully determined".'*

A number of quotations are attributed to Newman, but may not appear as verifiable in the accepted body of his work. Every effort has been made to ensure that the quotations and passages are actually the work of the author and to check them as carefully as possible.

The Power of Music

Cease, stranger, cease those witching notes,
The art of syren choirs;
Hush the seductive voice that floats
Across the trembling wires.

Music's ethereal power was given
Not to dissolve our clay,
But draw Promethean beams from heaven
To purge the dross away.

On Being a Rebel

If I were an Irish man, I should be (in heart) a rebel.

On Church Fathers leading Newman towards Catholicism

To be deep in history is to cease to be a Protestant.

(*An Essay on the Development of Christian Doctrine*)

A Parting Thought – the Last Things

I die in the faith of the one holy Catholic Apostolic Church. I trust I shall die prepared and protected by her sacraments, which our Lord Jesus Christ has committed to her, and in the communion of saints which he inaugurated when he ascended on high, and which will have no end. I hope to die in that Church which our Lord founded on Peter, and which will continue till his second coming.

I commit my soul and body to the most holy Trinity and to the merits and grace of our Lord Jesus, God incarnate, to the intercession and compassion of our dear Mother Mary; to St Joseph and St Philip Neri, my father, the father of an unworthy son; to St John the Evangelist; St John the Baptist; St Henry; St Athanasius, and St Gregory Nazianzen, to St Chrysostom and St Ambrose.

Also to St Peter, St Gregory I, and St Leo. Also to the great apostle, St Paul.

Also to my tender Guardian Angel, and to all angels, and to all saints.

And I pray to God to bring us all together again in heaven, under the feet of the saints. And, after the pattern of him, who seeks to diligently for those who are astray, I would ask him especially to have mercy on those who are external to the true fold, and to bring them into it before they die.

(*Passion Sunday, 13 March 1864*)

1. *Aberdeen Evening Express*, 12 August 1890.
2. *Cork Examiner*.
3. Cardinal Cahal B. Daly, *Blessed John Henry Newman: His Relevance for Today*.
4. Dessain, *John Henry Newman*, p. 169.

BIBLIOGRAPHY

PRIMARY SOURCES

Newman, John Henry, *Apologia Pro Vita Sua*, London: Longmans, Green & Co., 1891.

———, *Autobiographical Writings*, Henry Tristram (ed.), London: Sheed and Ward, 1956.

———, *An Essay on the Development of Christian Doctrine*, London: Longmans, Green & Co., 1914.

———, *Callista: A Tale of the Third Century*, London: Longmans, Green and Co., 1893.

———, *Certain Difficulties Felt by Anglicans in Catholic Teaching* (*Letter to the Duke of Norfolk*; *Letter to Rev. E.B. Pusey D.D.*) (2 vols), London: Longmans, Green and Co. 1894.

———, *Discourses Addressed to Mixed Congregations*, London: Longmans, Green and Co., 1897.

———, *Discussions and Arguments on Various Subjects*, London, Longmans, Green & Co., 1891.

———, *Essays Critical and Historical* (2 vols), London, Longmans, Green & Co., 1891.

———, *Essays on Miracles*, London: Longmans, Green & Co., 1890.

———, *Historical Sketches* (2 vols), London: Longmans, Green & Co., 1906.

———, *An Essay in Aid of a Grammar of Assent*, London: Longmans, Green & Co., 1898.

———, *Loss and Gain: The Story of a Convert*, London: Longmans, Green & Co., 1893.

———, *Meditations and Devotions of the Late Cardinal Newman*, London: Longmans, Green & Co., 1893.

———, *My Campaign in Ireland*, London: A. King and Co., 1896.

———, *On the Scope and Nature of University Education*, London: J.M. Dent and Sons, Ltd., 1915.

———, *Oxford University Sermons*, London: Longmans, Green & Co., 1892.

———, *Parochial and Plain Sermons* (8 vols), London: Longmans, Green & Co., 1894.

———, *Sermons on Subjects of the Day*, London: Longmans, Green & Co., 1891.

———, *The Arians of the Fourth Century*, London: Longmans, Green & Co., 1891.

———, *The Idea of a University*, London: Longmans, Green & Co., 1893.

———, *On Consulting the Faithful in Matters of Doctrine*, John Coulson (ed.), London: Geoffrey Chapman, 1961.

———, *Sayings of Cardinal Newman*, London: Burns & Oates, Ltd, c.1890.

———, *Sermons Preached on Various Occasions*, Longmans, Green & Co., 1908.

———, *Verses on Various Occasions*, London: Longmans, Green & Co., 1890.

PRAYER BOOKS

A John Henry Newman Prayer Book, London: St Pauls Publishing, 2010.

Heart to Heart: A Cardinal Newman Prayer Book, Notre Dame: Christian Classics, 2011.

GENERAL BIBLIOGRAPHY

Armstrong, Dave (ed.), *The Quotable Newman*, Manchester: Sophia Institute Press, 2012.

Beaumont, Keith, *Blessed John Henry Newman: Theologian and Spiritual Guide for Our Times*, Paris: Editions du Signe, 2010.

Boyce, Philip, *The Virgin Mary in the Life and Writings of John Henry Newman*, Herefordshire: Grace Wing, 2001.

Campion, Edmund, *John Henry Newman: Friends, Allies, Bishops, Catholics*, Melbourne: Dove Communications, 1980.

Chadwick, Owen, *Newman*, Oxford: Oxford University Press, 1983.

Chapman, Frederick, *The Poems of John Henry Newman*, London: John Lane, 1933.

Cornwell, John, *Newman's Unquiet Grave: The Reluctant Saint*, New York: Continuum, 2010.

Crosby, John F., *The Personalism of John Henry Newman*, Washington DC: The Catholic University of America Press, 2014.

Cunningham, Lawrence S. (ed.), *John Henry Newman: Heart Speaks to Heart: Selected Spiritual Writings*, New York: New City Press, 2004.

Daly, Cardinal Cahal B., *Blessed John Henry Newman: His Relevance for Today*, Armagh: Cumann Seanchais Árd Mhaca, 2010.

Dessain, C.S., *John Henry Newman*, Oxford: Oxford University Press, 1980.

———, *Newman's Spiritual Themes*, Dublin: Veritas Publications, 1977.

Dulles, Avery, *John Henry Newman*, New York, Continuum, 2002.

Elwood, J. Murray, *Kindly Light: The Spiritual Vision of John Henry Newman*, Indiana: Ave Maria Press, 1966.

Fathers of the Birmingham Oratory, *Sermon Notes of John Henry Cardinal Newman*, 1849–1878, London: Longmans, Green & Co., 1914.

Forristal, Desmond, *Newman in Dalkey*, n.d.

Gilley, Sheridan, *Newman and His Age*, London: Darton, Longman & Todd, 1990.

Holmes, J. Derek and Hugo M. de Achaval (eds), *The Theological Papers of John Henry Newman on Faith and Certainty*, Oxford: Clarendon Press, 1976.

Honoré, Jean, *The Spiritual Journey of Newman*, New York: Society of St Paul, 1997.

Ker, Ian, *John Henry Newman: A Biography*, Oxford: Oxford University Press, 1988.

——— (ed.), *John Henry Newman: Meditations and Devotions*, Toronto: Novalis, 2010.

———, *Newman on Being a Christian*, London: Harper Collins, 1990.

———, *The Genius of John Henry Newman: Selections from His Writings*, Oxford: Oxford University Press, 2012.

Mansfield, Dermot, *Heart Speaks to Heart: The Story of Blessed John Henry Newman*, Dublin: Veritas, 2010.

McGrath, Fergal, *Newman's University: Idea and Reality*, Dublin: Browne and Nolan, Ltd, 1951.

McRedmond, Louis, *Thrown Among Strangers: John Henry Newman in Ireland*, Dublin: Veritas, 1990.

Manser, Martin H., *The Westminster Collection of Christian Quotations*, Kentucky: Westminster Knox Press, 2001.

Martin, Brian, *John Henry Newman: His Life and Work*, London: Geoffrey Chapman Mowbray, 1990.

Maxwell, John C., *Developing the Leader Within You*, Nashville: Thoman Nelson, 1982.

Mozely, Anne (ed.), *Letters and Correspondence of J.H. Newman* (2 vols), London: Longmans, Green & Co., 1891.

Norris, Thomas J., *Cardinal Newman for Today*, Dublin: The Columba Press, 2010.

O'Carroll, Ciarán, *Catholic University Church*, Dublin: Newman University Church, 2010.

O'Faoláin, Seán, *Newman's Way*, London: Longmans, Green & Co., 1952.

O'Loughlin, Thomas, *Newman: A Religious Quest*, Dublin: Veritas, 2001.

———, *Cardinal Newman: Seeker of Truth*, Dublin, Veritas, 1988.

Rear, Michael, *Blessed John Henry Newman*, London: St Pauls, 2010.

Skinner, Gerard, *Newman the Priest: A Father of Souls*, Herefordshire: Gracewing, 2010.

Strachey, Lytton, *Eminent Victorians*, Oxford: Oxford University Press, 2009.

Strange, Roderick (ed.), *John Henry Newman: A Portrait in Letters*, Oxford: Oxford University Press, 2015.

Sugg, Joyce, *John Henry Newman*, London: The Incorporated Catholic Truth Society, 1986.

Trevor, Meriol, Newman: *The Pillar of the Cloud*, London: Macmillan and Co. Ltd, 1962.

Tyler, Mary (ed.), *John Henry Newman: Collected Poems and the Dream of Gerontius*, Kent: Fisher Press, 1992.

Ward, Maisie (ed.), J.H. Newman, *Apologia Pro Vita Sua*, London: Sheed & Ward, 1945.

Ward, Wilfrid, *The Life of John Henry Cardinal Newman* (2 vols), London: Longmans, Green & Co., 1912.

Velocci, Giovanni, *Prayer in Newman*, Pennsylvania: Newman House Press, Gracewing, 2004.

Paidir go John Henry Newman

A Naoimh John Henry Newman,

Chaith tú do shaol ag lorg na fírinne agus anois tá tuiscint iomlán agat ar cad atá i gceist.

Déan beagán de sholas na tuisceana sin a lonrú orainn, Pobal Dé in Íosa Críost.

Nuair atáimid ag cuartú sóláis agus muid thíos le héagóir agus báite san éadóchas,

déan gaoth úr a spreagadh agus a shéideadh inár seolta.

Cuir bac ar an mianach atá ionainn breithiúnas a thabhairt ar dhaoine eile.

Tabhair faoiseamh dúinn nuair atá olc orainn agus déan muid a tharrtháil

ó fharraigí garbha an fhrustrachais.

Stiúir go talamh slán muid le cuid de shíocháin idéalach Ríochta Dé.

Áiméan

Prayer to John Henry Newman

Dear Saint John Henry Newman,
You sought after truth and now you understand it perfectly.
Shine a little of that light of understanding on us your brothers and sisters in Christ.
Whenever we are becalmed and motionless in despair,
Inspire us with a gentle breeze to our backs.
Still our compulsion to judge others in the poorest of light.
Calm all our anger and save us
From the rough seas of frustration.
Lead us safely to port and a share in the perfect peace of God's Kingdom.
Amen.